All My Oceans

Poems: 1990—2020

Vera Nazarov

All My Oceans, Poems: 1990—2020

© 2023 by Vera Nazarov

All rights reserved. No part of this publication may be reproduced, distributed, or transmitted in any form or by any means, including photocopying, recording, or other electronic or mechanical methods, without the prior written permission of the copyright holder, except in the case of brief quotations embodied in critical reviews and certain other noncommercial uses permitted by copyright law.

ISBN: 9798395712981

Library of Congress Control Number: 2023910193

Cover Design by Vera Nazarov

Printed in the United States of America.

Published at San Jose, CA. June 2023

All My Oceans

To Roseanna, for showing me how.
To Evangela, for showing me why.
And to Sterling, for patience, good humor, and friendship.

*And if a god will wreck me yet again on the wine-dark sea,
I can bear that too, with a spirit tempered to endure.*
—Homer, *The Odyssey*

Table of Contents

Wine-Dark Sea
On Your Shore 3
Chameleon 5
Echoes 6
Heat 7
Dreaming of Red 8
How Love Comes 9
Gravity 10
Beauty 11

Sirens
Stained 15
Here, Now 17
Kiss 19
Submission 20
Fruta Prohibida 21
Juice 22
Things You Miss: A Litany 23
Places Seldom Kissed: A Litany 24
Cernunnos 26

Ring of Fire
Barren 29
Fishing 31
Castles in Spain 32
Grapes 33
Babies 34
Hair 35
Borders 36
Learning a Foreign Language 37
The Fisherman's Wife Writes to Her Friend 38
ICU 40
Old Bones 41
Feet 42
Becoming the Sun 43

Panthalassa

Equinox 47
Horse Daydreaming in a Sunny Field 48
Four Seasons Kanji 49
Rain 50
Tangerines 51
Migraine 52
The Cat's Snooze as an event in spacetime 53
Zen Garden 54
Stone in a Temple Wall 55

Tiamat

Today My Name Is… 59
The Quilters 60
Eucalyptus 61
Delta 62
Saturday Morning in the Group Home 64
Riding the Horse 65
Ballet Russe 66
Clocks 67
5 May 2010 69
    1. Collision 69
    2. On the Shoulder 70
    3. Ambulance 71
    4. ER 72
    5. Grace 74
Mining the Ore 75
Balancing Act 76

Tethys

The Visit 79
Feathers 81
Selfish Child 84
Wearing My Mother's Face 86
Things Fall Apart 88
A Gift of the Heart 89
Anchor 91
My Father's Kitchen 92
Several Attempts at a Funerary Poem 93
Father 95

Rusalka

A Little Heart to Heart	99
Persephone and Hades	100
A New Hester Prynne	101
Innocent Love is Easy Love	102
Ghosts	104
Falling	106
Boundaries	107
Mask	108
Closed Circuit	110
Incarnate	112
The Brutal Gentleness of Regret	113
Index of Titles	115
Index of First Lines	117

Wine-Dark Sea

On Your Shore

> *The heart can think of no devotion*
> *Greater than being shore to ocean—*
> *Holding the curve of one position,*
> *Counting an endless repetition.*
>   —Robert Frost, *Devotion*

Suppose your body was an ocean:
bright shining, sun-dappled radiance,
coruscating surface of a million
ephemeral diamond sparkles,
azure and gold shading to emerald,
deepening into indigo,
fading finally to the abyssal midnight of
your darkest secret,
your deepest shame.

Rock and coral, your bones;
shifting currents, the tug and stretch of muscle and sinew;
ebb and flow of tide, the pulse of your blood, your breath.

In the swift flicker of fish,
turning and wheeling,
the vibrant lightning of your thoughts;
your sadness, the lonely keening of sea birds;
your anger, sharks gliding like crimson knives
through storm-tossed waters,
rising red and dreadful
from the black miasma of nightmare.

Suppose before you could speak
your body had already,
by virtue of its restlessness,
rendered the elements of
sand and silt, drifting sea grass,
tang of salt, murmur of wave.
Suppose this unceasing motion of your body
was a soul-deep trembling as you lie with me.
What is the one true thing you do not know?
Lean into me...lean your blood and your wishes into my stillness
and listen—I'll tell you the secret at the heart of this dance.

I would be your coastline,
shore to your restless ocean,
welcoming the constant motion
of endlessly pounding surf rising
higher and higher, until
one final monstrous wave crashes
in torrents of released energy
and exploding spume.

And in the aftermath,
in the gentle ebb of your tide,
I would cradle you close,
hold you, as an enfolding bay
shelters calm waters at sunset...
safe harbor.

Chameleon

"Chameleon," he said,
"you're a poet, and poets lie."
Those words spoken casually
by a man, sunlight-golden,
with eyes blue as deep summer
as he leaned, hip cocked,
against the bed of a banged-up '64 Chevy pickup
in his bicep-bulging t-shirt,
low slung jeans, dusty work boots,
the hair on his arms glinting like some kind of halo.
This man whose throat muscles I'd silently worshipped
as he tilted his head back to drain the last of his *Corona*,
whose voice ran along my spine like hot lead
so I sometimes couldn't hear his words
for the thunder of my own blood,
whose hands could play me
like Casals his cello…Segovia his guitar,
who had once told me, quite seriously,
that trust was something to be earned, not freely given.
This man to whom I'd just said
"I love you."

I've come to believe, finally,
that he spoke more truth than he knew.
Poets lie,
like summer trees,
like winter trees.

Echoes

> *And for years I believed*
> *That what went unsaid between us became empty,*
> *And pure, like starlight, & that it persisted.*
>   —Larry Levis, *Winter Stars*

Voices beamed into space,
bounced off satellites,
millions of conversations creating a shell of words,
intricate, convoluted,
secret as the chambered heart of a nautilus,
sussurant buzz surrounding the planet,
as stars shine indifferently.
And out of this hazy halo of conversation,
out of all the mothers and daughters,
fathers and sons,
distant and star-crossed lovers,
your voice late at night,
drowsy and intimate in my ear.

Our midnight exchanges:
meandering tangles of thought given
breath, voice, life,
unfurl slowly, like night-blooming moonflowers,
draw us in like moths,
pollen heavy, drunk on nectar,
tongues, words, sweet as honey,
passion knotted,
entangling...entwining...

I think of our voices, our words,
somehow persisting...
some faint trace of us lingering
like the fragrance of a garden on the still night air,
thinning out across the emptiness between stars,
eventually, after billions of years,
filling the entire universe with
fragmentary traces of the love between us,
tenuous echo, half imagined,
caught by beings somewhere...somewhen...
who pause and momentarily wonder at this
ancient remnant of feeling,
at once so fragile and so primal.

Heat

Summer hills—
stone and bone clad in
blond velvet,
deep green feathering
of live oak and eucalyptus
beneath the still, clear sky.
And you there too:
taut whiteness—an opal or diamond
decoratively placed focus,
fulcrum,
the point of balance upon which
everything turns.

You are a boat,
billowing white sail against deep blue sky.
You cradle me close in the hollow
between your ribs and your hips,
safe harbor where I rock at anchor
in the amnion sea—deep as sleep,
lost in the mazarine maze
until your hands carry me up to the light,
and I'm born once again to your mouth whispering
a million delirious kisses.

I'm drowning,
drunk with the sun-sweat of you—
milk-languid,
honey-luscious,
moon-smooth peachskin
easy like the lazy sea.
Love's delicate apparatus:
lip tension and breath yielding
complexity of pattern,
frantic music beneath my fingers,
blood-flood I worship.

Summer may lick the mad rain from the sky,
but our storm will blow always.

Vera Nazarov

Dreaming of Red

Beneath the moon, beneath the trees,
in the street below my window,
I dreamt your face—the moon's reflection:
inverted, pallid,
camouflaged in a patchwork of leaf shadow—
your eyes, deep pools of tranquil water,
gazing up, but not toward me.
I rested my brow against the icy glass
and wept for all unspoken words, untaken chances,
mistaken and misspent hours and days…months and years.
The glass went misty with my breath,
then bled to black.

Because the day had been rushed,
and because my heart was broken,
I came home spent, heartsore, weary,
and slept until I thought I heard your heart…
spent, heartsore, weary,
calling to mine,
and woke happy in that moment
before the dream slowly died.

Lately I keep my heart in my pocket.
It's a sad, patched, threadbare old thing…
faded, frayed in odd places,
but soft and comforting to the touch.
Its hues, no longer vibrant, smolder with a pastel loveliness,
it aches with a lingering tenderness learned only after sorrow…
dying embers of a tenderness
I planned to wrap around you
like a warm quilt to keep you from the cold.

Some days disappear like rain in the desert…
evaporating before even touching the ground.
Some days last forever…
these days, without you, last forever.

I want to be more like the color red.
I want to shatter my black, break through your blue,
unfetter, unshackle, unloose, unchain…
clothe us both in radiant love.

How Love Comes

Infinite blue dome;
the eucalyptus on the hills
lift high their graceful branches—
toes rooted solidly in earth,
great arms clasping sun and air to their bosoms,
holding up the sky.

A small covey of quail darts around their roots,
bright-eyed,
topknots cheerfully bobbing,
while above a skein of larks flings itself joyfully
across the noon sky,
playfully weaves in and out of sunbeams.

I sit,
back against this tree,
hands splayed on this earth,
feet bare, toes immersed in this sea of grass.
Through every pore of my skin I inhale
this light,
this life,
and exhale love.

Gravity

The scented morning teases you awake:
cedar, floor-wax, sun-bleached linen.
The sun is a shout of heat
amid lemon trees and star jasmine.
Fragrance lies heavy on the still air.
Blinds hang precise and white,
strips of light and shade.

And this is all ordinary,
common as rain on a dusty road.

The woman you love arises amid sea foam—
night's tangled sheets—
gathering up her hair.
The flamenco curve of her back
is sheened with sweat
in the oppressive heat—
August, late morning.

She speaks of ordinary things:
coffee and oranges, the newspaper,
her voice a drowsy murmur of bees.

You see the marks of your hands,
love's stigmata,
faint tracery of purple on her thighs
and you are hurled into the world again,
victim of the law of gravity,
the gravity of love.

Beauty

I know that I am not beautiful.
My waist is too wide,
thighs too thick, hips too heavy
for beauty's measure.
My face: pure Slavic peasant—
blunt, inelegant, plebeian—
lacks the patrician planes,
aristocratic angles,
that beauty requires.

But when I lie beneath you
and my pale skin blossoms, glows,
rose-pink deluge surging like sunrise
in quivering response to your touch;
when my mouth surrenders its sweetness
in lingering, clinging kisses,
sensitive flesh delicately abraded
by the sandpaper rasp of your chin;
when you hover above me—sky over earth—
then, hawklike, stoop…plummet…descend…
collapse into me, a shockwave of lightning
vibrating throughout your body,
all your radiance, your strength, your intensity
gathered in a knot at the base of your spine,
urging…compelling your fierce motion;
when the sinewy strength of your thighs pinions mine
and your tousled head lies pillowed
on the tender softness of my breast;
when your dark eyes are rapt, adrift,
drowning in my ocean-blue gaze—
spellbound, sinking stonelike into the sea
of my profound adoration…
am I not lovely?
Do I not then
become beautiful?

Sirens

Stained

> *I crave the stain*
>
> *Of tears, the aftermark*
> *Of almost too much love...*
>   —Robert Frost, To Earthward

To be stained,
every inch of me,
with you...

A whisper of warm breath in my ear.
Moist trails of kisses you sow along my neck,
harvesting a flush of heat,
capturing the breath of my gasp,
moan, with your lips.
Our mingled sweat,
slick slide of skin,
and that other warm slickness
you find first with questing fingers,
then your mouth...
The muscles of my thighs quiver—
marionettes, clumsily mimicking
the cadence of your dancing tongue.

I am a bush of *Ilex verticillata*,
winterberry holly,
ripe, hung with crimson fruit—
a bush of bells set ringing
by flocks of small birds
harvesting, harvesting...
each chime and shiver
a minute song of praise.

And when I am finally transfixed,
pierced, impaled,
and the fire runs along my bones,
burning, scorching,
as you pour yourself into me,
wine into a chalice...
then to be printed,
to wear the texture of your skin,
the imprint of each whorl of hair,
your fingerprints everywhere eclipsing
the vibrant flame of my presence,
to bear the mark and stain of you
forward into the world...

what need, anymore,
for clothes?

Here, Now

> *Now you grab me by the ankles.*
> *Now you work your way up the legs*
> *and come to pierce me at my hunger mark.*
>   —Anne Sexton, Barefoot

It is here that I wait for you always,
breathing without you,
breathing you in and out,
in this room where I inhale and exhale
alternating darkness and light,
the shyness in my eyes belied by
the metronome of blood that shivers my wrist,
measuring moments until your mouth brushes,
lightly as a moth,
my skin…the tender softness just there,
at the nape of my neck,
behind the shell of my ear,
in the bend of my elbow,
at the back of my knee,
as you discover the taste of me—
sweetness and salt, rising
to a high-tide watermark.

It is here that your warm breath,
the sweet seduction of your mouth,
make me close my eyes and sigh…
and it is here that the rasp of your teeth,
the tease of your tongue,
cause my flesh to rise and pucker,
straining toward more,
straining toward you…
and it is here that your lightest touch,
the merest brush of your fingertips
repeatedly along folds and creases,
results in an unfolding,
flushing,
burgeoning,
blossoming,
extravagant orchid,
dew-pearled,
fragrant…flagrant…

It is here that I lay my hands on your skin,
here that my fingertips blindly
trace the curve of your ear,
stroke the column of your throat,
blaze a trail down the plane of your chest,
across the arc of your belly,
parsing smooth from rough,
as my wanton mouth follows in abandoned praise.

It is here that the lion and lamb lie together.
Here alone, here all one.
Here always and in all ways.
Here, now,
it is here, it is here.

Kiss

> *when you kiss me, the rain falls thick as rubber,*
> *sunset pours red caramel down my spine*
> *and, in my hips, the green wings of the jungle flutter...*
> —Diane Ackerman, *Beija-Flor*

Kiss...kiss me...
Kiss me like your thirst is eternal—
    scorched, razed, desolate, desert dry—
    and my mouth is your only source of water.
Drink me.

Kiss me like you're drowning and my mouth is the surface of the ocean,
    my mouth is breath, my mouth is air.
Kiss me, and let our breaths, tongues, souls mingle.
Kiss me like moth wings, like hummingbird wings,
    like the silent wings of a hunting owl.
Kiss me—oh, yes—there!

Kiss me warm, kiss me luminous, kiss me radiant.
Kiss me pliant, kiss me bountiful, kiss me into surrender.
Kiss me dark, kiss me deep, kiss me drugged on your mouth.
Kiss me drunk with passion.
Kiss me wanting you.
Kiss me dazed, kiss me blind, kiss me crazy, kiss me stupid.
Kiss me until the entire world is the seam, the joining,
    the meeting of your mouth and my mouth.

Kiss me...just kiss me.

Submission

> *... por quien me olvido de esta existencia mezquina,*
> *por quien el día y la noche son para mí lo que quiere,*
> *y mi cuerpo y espíritu flotan en su cuerpo y espíritu*
> —Luis Cernuda, *Si el hombre pudiera decir lo que ama*

For you alone...
my two hands, cupping grace, dripping light,
bringing to lay at your feet my living heart;
tapering limbs for you to grasp, hold, encircle,
confine in leather, metal;
flutter of my butterfly tongue, steel-pinned—
odalisque,
writhing contortionist,
belly dancer with her jeweled navel;
my ghost skin, which remembers,
learns by heart in shades of crimson
every word you inscribe,
every rasp and abrasion of delicate flesh;
all my secrets laid bare...
each fragrant rise and damp hollow,
each breath and quiver,
each pout and pucker between
hip and lip.

These things I offer you,
kneeling at your feet,
your hand strong and sure at my nape,
your voice firm and commanding,
raising all the small hairs of my body
as I bend for you,
pliant as a reed.

You are the strength, the power...
the beam and brace of this shelter we build.
I, the gentle vine...
entwining, blossoming, casting shade.

I hold you in my delicate clasp
as you lift me up,
and together
we build this house.

Fruta Prohibida

Round sound of plum:
begins with a pout or pucker
leaves your lips,
lingering, loose and lovely,
on your tongue;
heart of plum parts your lips,
fills your mouth with words like
sun, luscious, love;
ends with a hum,
tickly buzz,
mmmmm.

Velvet bloom of peach:
sun-warm globe,
pale, blushing pink;
rosy firm softness of
skin stretched taut around
such summer sweetness.

Bloodstone cherry:
slippery-sweet flesh
tenderly enfolding
potential-energy pebble.

Melon belly:
deep pink heart alive with
millions of seeds.

Juice

> *Amazement is the thing.*
> *Not love, but the astonishment of loving.*
> —Alastair Reid, *Growing, Flying, Happening*

Sunlight dripped slowly, thick honey
from the serrated edges of live oak leaves—
green and gold striptease shimmy
of mile-high summer sky.
A coy little breeze danced,
hesitated,
danced again,
trailing indolent fingers over tall grasses
baking tawny-gold in the summer-scented air.

Then it all vanished.
The horizon contracted to the
boundary
between
your mouth and my fingers as you
licked the crimson stain of juice
from my skin.
Your kiss tasted of strawberries and wine.
My breath faltered,
caught in
the
odd
rhythm of
village music.

Things You Miss: A Litany

The sharp gasp she makes at your first thrust.
Her breath, warm on your skin,
    stirring the smallest hairs of your body.
The softness of her hands,
    touching, stroking, caressing, urging.
Her hungry mouth—feverish kisses
    along your jawline—insistent, begging for your mouth.
The heat of her surrounding you,
    clasping you, enfolding you.
Her hips, the cradle of her thighs,
    where you rock, anchored yet adrift
    in the warm salt sea of her.
Your name in all the ways she says it:
    whispering, pleading, gasping, sighing, exulting.
The storm that takes you as she cries out your name,
    shuddering beneath you, around you.
The calm following the storm,
    as you fall deep and deep into her softness,
    into the tenderness of her love for you,
    as she strokes your back in the absolute peace of fulfillment.

Places Seldom Kissed: A Litany

> *I took the one less traveled by,*
> *And that has made all the difference.*
> —Robert Frost, *The Road Not Taken*

Fingertips.
The hollow at the center of your palm.
Delicate web of skin between palm and thumb.
Crease of your wrist, where your pulse flutters—
    a frantic moth against the flame of my mouth.
Blue tracery of veins along your inner forearm—
    map your clamorous blood implores, impels me to follow.
Bend of your elbow: soft, vulnerable, ticklish.
Heavy strength of your bicep.
Armpit—dark, secret, redolent with your musk.
Shoulder top, which none but the sun has kissed
    until now.
Subtle incline between neck and shoulder.
Tender skin behind your ear.
Nape of your neck…when my breath feathers across it,
    all the small hairs of your body awake in supplication.
Twin planes of shoulder blades—hidden wings
    that shift and stiffen in anticipation of flight.
Strong column of spine—your body's scaffolding.
Small of your back, which urgently arches when we are joined,
    and shuddering, you fall fiercely into me.

Toes.
Arch of your foot—supple, elegant.
Ankle—flexible engine of tendon and bone.
Long flatness of shin.
Back of your knee—covert, isolated,
    it nonetheless quivers at the boldness of contact.
Inner thigh…when I kiss you here, your muscles twitch and shiver
    at the intimate audacity of my mouth.
Juncture of thigh and torso—major hinge of your body.
Linea alba… path my mouth follows to the valley of your navel…
    over the slope of your belly.
Sternum—densely haired breastplate that guards your heart.
    I kiss it in praise of its purpose.
Mirrored collarbones—twin wings gracefully framing your neck,
    the stalk of your face.

Suprasternal notch—the hollow of your throat,
    where your voice vibrates the torrent of your breath.
Bottom of your chin, blunt projection that I ascend,
    leaving a string of kisses as trail markers.
Shallow hollow of the crease below your lips.
Corners of your mouth, where your smiles live
    sleeping until they're kissed awake.
Upper planes of your cheekbones.
Your eyelids, closed now in entreaty.

Cernunnos

He stands too still for me to perceive,
vanishing into leaf mould, fernbrake.
His eyes surrender to the twilit sky
the darkness that pools beneath spectral trees.
His pale skin changes, goes dusky, strange,
mottled with leaf shadow, moon-dappled.

He leaves no trace where he passes,
no snapped twig, turned stone,
no rain-filled dimple of foot or hoof,
only the fleeting heat of a brief hand
lingering on tree bark, heartwood,
a rumor of dew scattered from subtly disturbed grass.

I stand in bright moonlight, naked, exposed,
blinded, eyes dazzled, powerless to stir foot,
rooted, bound, muscles taut, quivering—
prey that has winded the hunter,
but knows not where to run,
which way to turn…

Strange man, stag man,
come to me beneath the blood moon—
rain and wind, the scent of your skin,
loam and flame, the taste of your mouth.
Soft and slow as moss, your shadow hands stray over my bones.
Your breath on my skin: a stream of liquid fire.

Stag-man, hunter,
come for me across the pale, misted fields,
clothed in darkness, trailing silence behind you.
I wait for you, bound yet willing.
I will be your threefold sacrifice:
    bludgeoned—your touch kills my thought…
    strangled—your mouth steals my breath…
    drowned—I sink wordlessly into your whirlpool heart.

Hunter, horned man,
with eyes like the wild stag,
gather the hunt, loose the hounds,
chase my heart across the wild winter sky.

Ring of Fire

Barren

...in which the poet does not rejoice to see the end of a drought.

I was becoming used to this serene emptiness—
the strange, lunar beauty of austere landscapes,
black branches stark against a brazen sky,
hills dry and barren,
no cloud in sight,
no breath of wind,
no scent of rain;
restful as a monastery:
cloistered paths warm and dusty,
muted bells chiming ritual hours,
three handfuls of parched corn
and a bowl of goat's milk by candlelight,
the wine cellar's flagstones
cool beneath my feet.

No tangled green riot
of sticky young leaves,
no reek of hot blood
and that little death
when the silken cords are cut
and life takes, once again, its first breath.

But the Pythia returns,
always.
She comes from the east, bearing strange gifts:
branch of almond blossom,
husk of albino cobra,
flowering thistle,
skull of an owl.
Her eye sanctifies my brow
with a fever of yearning,
fills with radiance that strange dark place
where she kneels, whispering forbidden secrets,
amid the mist that rises
from my dreams.

"Go away." I told her.
"I have learned to live without your touch;
my heart no longer blooms like a rose
to feed your frenzied dances."
Her answer is silence;
her eyes, deep wells of black water.

I fall endlessly.

She touches my face
and promises much rain.

Fishing

It's like waking up
and finding yourself at a half-remembered riverbank,
pole in hand,
cold worms
wriggling out of an old soupcan,
smell of rotting leaves and long-dead mice,
mud squishing up between your toes;

just barely morning,
the last few stars winking up at you
from backwater pools,
ghosts of mist catching the first sallow traces
of false dawn,
poking clammy ashen fingers
between twisted black roots of fallen trees.

The tip of your pole dips slightly
so slightly, you hesitate—
and you peer, eyes narrowed against the dark,
breath caught behind your teeth—
there again, it dips;
a faint vibration shivers your wrist
and you hear the pale sigh of trout gulping air.

This is the sound you follow
to the root of your mind
and deeper
sinking, tunneling,
following its elusive golden thread
until you find yourself
back here,
alone
on this riverbank,
hook shining,
breath bated,
and the silver flicker
of the almost possible
disappearing.

Castles in Spain
(for Evangela)

> De Guiche: Car lorsqu'on les attaque, il arrive souvent...
>
> ...
>
>   Qu'un moulinet de leurs grands bras chargés de toiles
>   Vous lance dans la boue!
>
> Cyrano: Ou bien dans les étoiles!
>
> —Edmond Rostand, *Cyrano de Bergerac*

I've never been to Spain,
yet I know how sunlight scatters
showers of ancient gold
across the dusty *Plaza del Toros*,
and how the bright blood
singing with life
seeps slowly into golden sand
while a great black bull
snuffles at the fallen matador.

I know how indigo dusk
spills from the lips of
low-throated *abuelas*
stitching wedding linen
beneath the olive trees—
how it gathers and spreads
in cool blue pools
across the silent valleys—slowly rising
finally to engulf the gold-crowned mountains.

Until even here, in this gold-green valley
of Spain-kissed California
I feel myself gathered in, enfolded,
drawn to the sky's edge,
spilled over into darkness,
and I am once again
La Mancha and his windmills:
tilting,
always precariously
tilting.

Grapes

Hunched over in the dusty California sunlight
migrant workers move up
and down the rows of grapes
carefully cutting,
tenderly cupping each handful
of juice and skin.

Table grapes must be handled gently,
never bruised…
they learn to move among them by touch,
callused hands finding the clustered bunches
hidden under the leaves like
lines of braille.

The vine frames shudder in syncopated rhythm
as the workers cup the grapes,
cut the stems with a flick of the knife,
lay the grapes gently in battered crates.
Their faces grow sweat-sticky
under brightly colored bandanas;
the knives catch their knuckles,
scattering drops of brilliant crimson
among the green clusters.
Each small breath of wind
becomes a blessing.

In the evening,
the grapes,
washed clean,
will be carelessly placed in clean wooden bowls
by people with soft white hands
while the farm workers bolt their coarse suppers—
rice and beans and corn tortillas—
and then sleep,
dreaming in stilted English
of tomorrow's fields.

Babies

I never wanted one,
or at most wanted one as a child wants—
a doll, a ball, a shiny new toy,
something to dress up, then fling
into a corner,
forgotten
until the next game.

But really, I never wanted one for myself,
content for friends to have them,
happy enough to hand the bundle back
before the wrapping came off
and the thing inside appeared,
lumpy and wet,
squalling with its wide red mouth,
a well of want.

Hot little body kicking damply in its cuddle-sack,
a cul-de-sac,
a screaming wet dead end.

Hair

It is sometimes a barrier
between me and the world;
autumn colors of ancient tapestries,
gossamer veils,
curtains of amber beads.

Then again, it is a net
in which to trap you;
silky strands to twine around your hands,
dragging you down,
pulling you deep beneath the flickering
shimmering surface
of my eyes.

It is my prison;
the rope you knot around my neck,
the chain you anchor around your wrist
tugging me toward you
when I would be off and running —
the string on a child's balloon.

I stumble over it.
Unbound,
it trails the floor.
Yet you are caught in it
as surely as I,
and we drown together.

Borders

People cross borders
even if they're not going anywhere —
not going anywhere particular.
The line you draw in the dust is a dare to cross it.

You set boundaries
knowing they will be violated —
fearing yet welcoming the one who suddenly appears,
quietly places a hand on your arm,
speaks words familiar and frightening.

People cross all borders.
Walls won't stop them.
Pain won't stop them.
Running away will only bring you to other people —
walls and pain won't stop them either.

Better to stop running,
turn back,
cross borders yourself,
accept the heavy ache of human touch —
the warm heaviness of a hand in your hand,
a stone dropped into a pool of water,
the changer and the changed.

Learning a Foreign Language

How the tongue struggles at first,
tripping over unfamiliar sounds —
vowels, consonants — never a consonance.
And the mind,
stubbornly thinking in English
"the pen, the pencil,
my aunt Matilda…"
Until one day,
like a swift sunrise,
*"la plume, le stylo,
ma tante Mathilde…"*
come easily,
naturally,
like breathing.

Fluency, however,
does not promise familiarity.
Formality lingers,
resisting the effortless *tutoyer*.
No longer a tourist, perhaps,
yet never a native —
forever a traveler,
prone to mishap,
malaprop,
the dreaded unknown idiom,
stubborn tics of
determinedly English syntax,
blind to passing wit,
innuendo,
the chance utterance of a graceful phrase.
Always wondering
what might be lost in translation.

The Fisherman's Wife Writes To Her Friend

You asked in your last letter
why I continue to live in a house I hate.
I don't hate this house.
I came here a child, a bride,
grew into a woman here.
I've lived in this house so long
it's like an old coat, a second skin.
I carry it with me everywhere,
like a turtle or a snail.
But I hate how everything smells of the sea,
how the blowing sand gets in everywhere.
You remember that story we read,
about a Japanese village being swallowed by the dunes,
and how the people worked day in and day out
shoveling the sand away—
they finally had to haul it up in buckets, it got so high around them.
I feel like that sometimes,
but it's not the sand, not really,
coming down on top of everything;
it's the memories, I guess.
I can't even walk down to the docks any more.
Do you remember how we used to sit down there for hours?
We'd come home reeking of fish and pitch,
with chapped hands and faces,
hair such a tangle of wind and spindrift
we'd have to wash it twice.
These days just the smell of fish makes me seasick.
Maybe that's it—sea-sickness, I mean.
I'm sick of the sea, but I continue to live here,
within spitting distance of it.

All My Oceans

He was still soaking wet when they brought him home;
so cold—blue with cold, or maybe that was lack of air.
I felt I was drowning too.
The sweater I knitted for him trailed little salty rivulets all over the floor—
tears I couldn't weep.
The sea was his great love
and she finally took him from me.
For that I can never forgive her.
It'll be two years next month.
So I guess I live here so I can see her wild face every day,
so she can know the hurt and harm she's done me,
and so I'll never again be fooled by the gentle face she puts on
for other people, other places.

ICU

Your body no longer belongs to you:
it is a foreign country you are visiting —
you don't speak its language;
you surrender it to the hands of strangers.
It has become a god in a macabre temple,
its rites administered by strange priests who murmur incessantly:
"Lave here; scatter flowers there;
inhale this incense, imbibe these consecrated waters."

The endless ritual does not permit sleep.
Indeed, your body, as the god, *must not* sleep.
Around the clock, deft machines capture each heartbeat, each breath;
each pulse of life is recorded, measured, quantified...

Time loses all meaning;
you begin to assess its passing by activity level:
it is noisier during the light,
you are disturbed more during the dark.

Your body has abandoned you to go sightseeing,
left you stranded on the side of the road.
You've bought a ticket,
boarded this ramshackle train...
there's no getting off.

Old Bones

> *I wish I had died young, suddenly,*
> *before I knew I had to make*
> *the bones of my soul*
> *out of cold rain and aching,*
> *and walk into the dark.*
> —Ursula K. Le Guin, *"Bone Poems" from Always Coming Home*

Old bones, you have danced
when I thought I could only weep.
You have carried me
places my soul never dreamed of walking.
You have taken me beyond the dreams of my mothers,
the grasp of my fathers,
beyond the furthest stone I ever threw.
You have trespassed in Coyote's house,
stolen fire from Raven,
when I had no way to warm you.
Now you are content to sit and tell
stories of water and earth and
cold sky dreaming.

Feet

The bottoms of your feet are soft and blind,
blunt as a dog's nose.
Your toes curl under,
curl into themselves—
fat little piggies,
pink where they're not pale.
They remember your babyfat laughter
floating up,
filling the sky with
bajillions of cloudnine bubbles
when your mama tweaked them,
telling you what they'd been up to
(one had been to market,
one had stayed home...)
when you weren't looking.

Feet are shy,
bundled in socks,
skulking in the caves of your shoes.
They come out when no one's watching,
deliberate as turtles,
slow as snails,
shedding, like snakes,
crumpled tubes of stockings.
They take pleasure in the textures of your floors:
chenille shag and tile,
plush berber,
smooth hardwood,
cool linoleum.
They want to dance naked on wet sand,
dew-damp grass.
They want to dance
naked
under the stars.

Becoming The Sun

The lion that lives in your garden,
drowsing in your daisies,
lounging amid the lobelia,
rufous mane a riot of roses and begonias,
saunters lazily about,
pokes his nose into honeysuckle shadows.
The geraniums make him sneeze.

Fiercely purring, entwined in strands of jasmine,
he sprawls sunward, belly up.
His inverted gaze considers
the pale softness of your feet,
toes curling in the dew-wet grass
beneath the pure white floating
of your linen shift.

You kneel…bury your fingers
in the silky corona surrounding his face.
His haunches shift, tail tip quivers,
as massive paws settle on your shoulders,
draw you chest to chest, belly to belly.
His warm outbreath flutters a leaf of peony,
ruffles your hair as you
snuggle into his rough fur.
You inhale the feral scent of him,
mouth open, tasting his musk—
it soaks into your skin,
absorbed by your pores.
A tawny wildness plummets deep into your heart
as he gently vanishes.

When you wake once again,
you gaze upon the world with golden eyes.

Vera Nazarov

Panthalassa

Vera Nazarov

Equinox

Now it is time for bluebells to sleep,
waiting for spring,
for love's first kiss.
It is time for bare bones of hazel
to skitter on cold windows
and for mountains to be fog-
wrapped and
solitary.

Unwind the wind.
Let it howl like a lost soul in its rustic asylum.
Let rain gently fall,
to wash away all that clings and besmirches.
Let the wild birches and aspen
breathe for a space
before winter blows in with icy breath,
piles snow on snow
to burn away all that is left.

Horse Daydreaming in a Sunny Field

I'm a fragment of river
whirling and spinning,
a leaf drifting on the scent of green.
When I run, my name is *Thunder*.
I snake my neck out, ears laid back;
there are teeth in the end.
You'd better watch your butt
you silly new filly.

I'm rooted solidly in earth,
each leg a tree
swaying over the small lives in this sea of grass.

I'm a piece of sky,
a word spoken by sunlight.
The electric shudder of my skin
sends the flies spiraling away with tiny hotfeet.
I horsewhip them midair with my tail.

I see you walking up behind me with that halter.
Come a little closer and get a taste of my heels.

Four Seasons Kanji

spring

wildflowers, grass, trees —
wind and rain paint subtle shapes,
letters to the earth.

summer

pond — golden koi knots
slowly form shadow letters
beneath mirrored blue.

autumn

leaves drift, copper, gold,
into bonfires...smoke rises —
letters, gray on gray.

winter

brush of tailfeathers,
blackest ink...a skein of crows,
cold paperwhite sky.

Rain

A million individual
pitter-pat footsteps,
unrelenting roar of a downpour,
a cat's purr in your ear,
gear-box of blood and air,
rare as breath, a flood,
a clot, flotsam from a wrack
of cloud, a veil, a shroud,
a winding sheet
three sheets to the unkind wind.

Strange precipitate,
super-saturate solution,
dissolute harbinger of death,
liquid thunder
from a mad god's anvil.
A wreath of water,
lovely daughter of the moon,
loon's lonely laughter,
numbing chatter of unnumbered
pitter-patter voices

Tangerines

ice-cold from the fridge
the first taste is on the breath
as you dig into the peel and the bitter oils burst free

and after the last juicy section has slipped silkily down
bitterness lingers at the back of your throat
the scent of citrus on your fingers

Migraine

Morning cracks
black as a headache
tasting of leaves and wet earth.
Splinters of light dance
in oil-slick colors
on the edges of your vision:
broken prisms,
shards of rainbow-hued ice,
dig into your eyes,
ride the optic nerve to the Stygian center,
to the pit where you dance naked
around your pillar of pain.
The only possible relief:
sleep blacker than death
curled in a fetal knot around the last pill
in the bottom of a prescription bottle.

The Cat's Snooze,
as an event in space-time

> *A sun far off in a shell of silence*
> *Dapples my walls for me...*
> —Conrad Aiken, Morning Song of Senlin

Nibbler of minutes,
devourer of hours,
you yawn hugely
and sleep slides down your pink gullet.
You curl yourself around nothing,
a furry torus.
The sun is pulled down into your well of sleep
and the afternoon becomes one giant event horizon.

You complain softly as you half-wake
(slitted eyes gleam star fire for an eternity of seconds)
then you sigh and resettle.
Galaxies swing grandly around you
as you sink once more into darkness.
The afternoon settles easily into its new pattern
and clocks and pendulums tick and swing
in rhythm with your purring.

Zen Garden

"It needs a gardener," I thought.
Tangled strands of bull kelp,
ripped from its mooring,
rooted in air, attached nowhere,
packed in random clumps.
Tiny crabs trapped in its strands—
a dance of frantically waving
snipping pincers.
Sand raked smooth by the summer tide
slowly flowing around
clean gray boulders.
A hundred miles of coastline
like a Japanese sand garden.
Perhaps it doesn't need a gardener.

Stone in a Temple Wall

I came from a mountain quarry.
Cut free of my mother, I was carried west
in a cart of fragrant pine.
Set down, I have not been moved since,
but have lain here while around me
empires have risen and fallen.

People move past me through alternating dark and light.
They touch me sometimes
and I feel the ebb and flow of their blood, their breath,
hear for a moment the undercurrent of mind;
their impermanence,
which they understand only as a rabbit understands the snare,
saddens me.

The shamen of this place have no deeper understanding.
Babies are brought here
who come back as husbands,
who come back as fathers,
who come back as corpses.
The shamen bless them and bless them and bless them
and place them in the ground;
then the worms and beetles are blest for a time.

Although my memory is long,
I have been a stone in this wall
almost longer than I can remember.
Dust from pilgrims' feet and calls to prayer have sunk into me
until I have become as holy as the gods who do not listen.

Sometimes in the clarity of morning
my mountains call to me.
I would go back, if I could,
to those places where the sacred yet lives —
chattering gullies amid fern fronds and pine boughs
where owl calls ride on the lowering dusk
and rabbits go to death innocent of snares,
where the glow in the golden eyes of elk
slowly deepens and dies
as a falcon's cry knifes through the still air.

I would like to begin again:
become water, brimming with life,
reflecting holy light, holding the moon in my liquid grasp.
The passage of time would bring me tales
of dew and ice-melt in the far peaks,
of plump, wet-muzzled deer standing in swift currents,
learning the scent of the night,
of deep places where the ancient dark is never broken,
until finally I became a still pool,
reflecting clouds
and pale branches of white birch.

Tiamat

Today My Name Is...

Today my name is *Heart's Thunder*.
Yesterday my name was *Mouse*.
I am a reed
bending with wind and water.
If you know how to place your fingers, your mouth,
where to blow a liquid stream of breath across my skin
you can make music.
Tomorrow I will be *Wind-Over-Water*.

My mother thought my name was *Gives Away*.
My father thought my name was *Keeps*.
I am a woven fish-basket
set under a cascade ledge.
I give away the silver-flickering river that flows through me.
I keep the silver-flickering fish.

The Quilters

We move like needles
through each other's lives:
mending, embroidering,
placing carefully
the colorful stitches.

We bring small gifts:
apricot mornings
awash with hope and daffodils,
small blue bowls of peace.

Our hands are busy always,
potting a plant…
plotting a birthday.

We are drawn together
by the geometry of our lives,
attentive always to the shapes and colors
we fuse between us as bridges.

Eucalyptus

> *Time held me green and dying*
> *though I sang in my chains like the sea.*
> —Dylan Thomas, *Fern Hill*

There is room tonight
beneath this sheltering sky
for the child I was then,
and for my brothers—
small, wiry boys with doe-shy eyes
and freckles smeared with summer dust.

It was always dusty under the trees there,
and the moonlight sifted through the leaves,
casting flickering shadows on our parched skin
(salty from the day's heat
amid the foxtails and scrub oak
of a California summer)
as we lay breathing the soft
eucalyptus air.

We slept there
in the deep hush of midsummer
as the moon sailed all uncaring overhead,
and we, swimming like fishes
amid the chains that bound us, each to each,
we slept there,
under the stars.

*

My brothers,
my wild ones,
we were not to know that summer would end,
sending me down a blood trail
you could not follow,
sending you into muscles and velvet voices,
sending us out and away—
three separate meteor-streaks
across the sky—
sending us out and forever away
from three children
sleeping under eucalyptus trees.

Vera Nazarov

Delta

The way my sister lolled at poolside:
head flung back under a sunshade of blonde-haloed arm,
one knee bent, the other
foot idly kicking in the water,
drawing the eye up her long white expanse of thigh
to the small delta of pink string bikini.

She ate ice cream, caressing it with her quick pink tongue,
letting the cool vanilla white slip down her throat,
ignoring the hot melting testosterone glares
that followed the final convulsive swallow
down to the hollow of her throat
where her sweat pooled,
cooled.
She knew, and knowing, laughed
at the mesmerized boys
caught in the endless loop of kick, thigh, pink.

She never swam, appearing on the scene
oiled and glistening, queenly regal.
In the heat of the day the water winked invitingly,
but to swim was to surrender one's body
to those who lurked underwater,
swimming by to snatch a feel
then fleeing, cool as seals, but burning hotter.

I, a sister, and much younger,
on the fringes of the communal shower,
saw what was coveted and covered:
an inverted triangle, v-shaped,
migratory delta-wing downed with hair.

I compared myself to my sister and her friends:
older girls all,
high-breasted,
little hairy triangles glistening with water droplets
as they blushed and giggled among themselves;
and to my mother:
full-blown, exotic, expansive,
brown as earth, plowed and planted,
juicy and warm as Seville oranges,
salt and sea, damp river delta.
I was a stick-straight body and naked little quim
(as yet only something to pee out of).
I didn't get it.

We walked home in the early evening,
my sister and I,
wearing shorts and halters,
flimsy rubber flip-flops slapping the cracked pavement.
The old men on the porches stared like the young boys.
She never looked at them, held me by the hand and walked on,
but she knew all the same, and knowing, smiled.
It was all a game, and she was winning.
She had an ace in the hole.

Vera Nazarov

Saturday Morning in the Group Home

The fourteen-year-old boy who raped a six-year-old girl
slouches on the couch, watching cartoons.
He calls the fat girl "Mama Cass,"
tells her to get out from in front of the TV—
she makes a better door than a window.

No one has figured out yet that the fat girl needs glasses.
She doesn't know either.
She's in the fourth grade and her world has always been incoherent.

The boy whose parents live in a drunken stupor
comes tearing downstairs naked,
twanging his penis like a tiny guitar.
He doesn't exist if he isn't yelled at daily.

The silent boy screams blue murder from the time-out box.
At five years old, he has no words.
The only tears he has left are tears of rage.
Last week he put his fist through a window and almost bled to death.
He never cried.

The blind girl sits on the floor
playing with a red plush horse and humming tunelessly.
Everyone is tired of telling her to shut up.

The counselors clatter around in the kitchen,
clearing up the spilled milk and breakfast cereal.
The male counselor likes the girl with breasts a little too much,
but he's careful and she's too young to understand
why she feels "icky" when he hugs her.

Outside, butterflies are fluttering in the sunlight,
bees are assaulting the lilac blossoms,
the backyard grass needs mowed.

Later today, we'll all go on an outing,
maybe to Alum Rock Park.
The older boys will toss a football back and forth.
The girls will sit on the swings and gossip.
The small fry will chase each other screaming through the creek.
We'll all desperately pretend to be normal,
even though none of us are very good at it.

Riding the Horse

Ragged thunderheads
and the shimmer and brilliance of rain
ghosting down sunlit canyons,
bright and soft as a lover's breath.

T-shirt clinging to new breasts,
shy as lilies.
The itch of dust and sweat
and short, sharp horsehairs
grinding through denim,
tickling the pale, soft insides of thighs.

Taste of salt,
and windblown earth.
Sting of sweat running into eyes.

Small neat feet
kicking up puffs of dust—
nothing but a pair of ragged jeans
between me and the horse,
and the hard ache of thighs
unused to parting,
unused to feeling a body,
hot and sweat-slick,
plunging like a diver
between them.

The summer I learned the difference
between horses and ponies.

Ballet Russe

Try to move me one inch I do not choose to move.
Generations of peasant women
have gone into my making,
each one planted like a tree,
stubborn as roots and rocks,
stones and bones.

Women did the work of horses in Russia.
I've seen pictures—gangs of women roped together
hauling canal barges upriver,
thighs thick like tree trunks,
hips broad and fruitful as fields of dark earth,
hands thickened from constant work,
skin burned dark by sun and wind.

My hands are soft,
white and fine,
fingers expensively perfumed and lacquered,
but scratch the surface and you'll find the thick bones
hard head of my *muzhik* father.

Fighting the genes of a million Russian *babushkas*:
Canute trying to command the sea.
I look at all the nervous little salad girls
and think to myself
a hundred generations of evolution can't be all wrong.

Clocks

Purpling like a bruise, the sky sleeps.
Darkness seeps from me like a pool
of black ink… Because I am a woman,
because my body vibrates to the clock
of all my blood's navies, all my bones'
scars and traces of grace on these white sheets

of paper—tearing at the sky—these sheets
cage my heart's fierce leaping. My blood sleeps.
I hear its whoosh and murmur in my bones,
feel it seep, gather, spread—a pool
of all that's sacred. It has been my clock
since the red day that I became a woman.

And just for that—because I *am* a woman,
because you find me soft between the sheets,
my heartbeat ticking, ticking, like the clock
that drives the green world, while the green world sleeps
and all its glory curdles in a pool
of gray milk—paste of ground-up bones,

you think you have the right, bred in your bones,
to cage me, keep me, tie me down; a woman
after all, is something owned—a pool,
a car, a house—anchor when you're three sheets
to the wind—tender ghost that sleeps
beside you, muffling the incessant clock.

I write so I can hear the ticking clock,
so I can feel time passing in my bones
while the indifferent world drifts and sleeps.
I write to know myself as every woman
I am—incline to naming on these sheets,
tracing my lineage from the farthest pool

of insight, the first life in some slimy pool
that knew itself as life and sparked the clock
that drives the force in me to cover sheets
of paper with the stories in my bones,
stories of millions, stories of every woman
before the clock is silenced and she sleeps.

Rising from my bones, a shallow pool
spreads to drown the clock that is the woman
in me. Mumbling in the sheets, he sleeps.

5 May 2010

1. Collision

You can see it's inevitable.
There's nothing you can do to prevent it.
It doesn't sound like you expect—
no slow motion cascade of ripping metal,
rippling force—
a dull thump, and your body hits a wall of "Stop!"
Airbags explode, faster than your brain can process—
you only see their limp, spent shapes when it's over.
Your car rolls to a stop in the service lane.
You calmly put it in park,
set the emergency brake,
turn off the ignition.
There is smoke,
an acrid chemical smell.
The horn is blaring.
There are other cars, other people,
more or less damaged.
Your door won't open.
You see traces of blood on it.
You remember a second impact.
You wait.
People ask you if you're ok—
you tell them "yes."
Your calm seems surreal to you.
Somewhere behind that wall of calm,
a part of your mind is screaming.

A highway patrol officer arrives.
He asks if you're ok.
He asks if your car can still move.
You're not sure, but you try the ignition.
It starts, and he tells you to drive over to the right shoulder,
then walks out onto the freeway to stop traffic.
You are surprised he isn't killed.
As you limp your car across the freeway
it groans in protest, but it moves.
Other cars are dragged across the freeway.
Traffic starts moving again.

2. On The Shoulder

The officer comes back,
tries to open your door.
It won't move.
He says he'll have to call the fire department.
He asks for your driver's license—you give him your wallet.
He asks you what happened.
You describe the accident.
Another officer comes.
He asks you what happened.
You describe the accident.
Other people start arriving—
firefighters, paramedics, tow-truck drivers.
You gather your personal belongings.
A firefighter tries to pry your door open with a hand tool.
It doesn't budge, and he walks away.
People keep asking if you have any pain in your neck,
in your back.
You keep telling them "no."
Someone tells a paramedic there's no c-spine.
The firefighter returns with a motorized tool.
You've never seen one before
but you know it's the "jaws of life."
His frail, human hands now wield the strength of a giant.
The door is gradually pried open
in a slow motion cascade of ripping metal,
rippling force.
It groans and screams in protest.
Metal loudly buckles and pops.
You feel afraid.

The firefighter asks if you can walk—you tell him "yes."
As you get out of the car, hands move to steady you.
Someone takes your backpack.
You glance at the door—
it's become a web of fragile, chaotic lace.
You can see its internal structure of struts and bars.
You feel afraid again.

An officer hands you your wallet back.
He asks for an alternate address, a telephone number,
your insurance policy number, your car registration.
You tell him the registration is in the glove compartment.
He asks you what happened.
You describe the accident.
You're surrounded by people, all asking you questions.
The paramedics are trying to move you towards the waiting ambulance.
The questions won't stop.
The questions come from all sides,
all together, all at once
hammering at you.
You feel a piece of glass in your shoe.
You shake it out as you try to answer the questions.
The officer gives you a collision report card,
a business card for the towing company.
Someone else has your backpack.
You have no pockets.
You try to remember to hold on to the cards.

3. Ambulance

The paramedics walk you to the ambulance,
help you inside,
tell you to sit/lie on the gurney.
They ask you which hospital you want to be taken to.
They take your vitals—pulse, heart, breath sounds.
They ask you to remove your sunglasses so they can check your pupils.
You'd forgotten you were wearing them.
They ask you if you lost consciousness—you tell them "no."
They check you over for injuries,
remove your shoes,
ask you to wiggle your toes, your fingers.
Everything seems to be working.
They ask you what happened.
You describe the accident.
You worry that they'll forget to bring your shoes.
At the hospital, they wheel you out.
One of them places your shoes on the gurney.
You feel relieved.

4. ER

The nurse at the admit desk asks for your medical record number three times.
You answer her each time.
She asks your name, your address, your phone number.
You suppose she's verifying you are who you claim to be.
You're taken to a room,
moved to another gurney.
You wait.

A nurse comes, gives you a gown, tells you to strip to the waist.
A few minutes later she hooks you up to a monitor—
heartbeat, respiration rate, blood pressure, blood oxygen level.
She asks you what happened.
You describe the accident.
She says you're lucky, but you know that.
She asks you if you lost consciousness—you tell her "no."
You tell her you remember the entire accident.
She says maybe you'd rather have lost consciousness.
She bandages a scrape on your arm,
brings you a blanket,
says she'll try to find you a pillow,
says the doctor will be in shortly.
You wait.

A maintenance worker comes in to empty the biohazard bin.
He says hello, asks you about your tattoos.
As he leaves, you notice he walks with a limp.
You wait.

The doctor comes, listens to your chest.
She asks you what happened.
You describe the accident.
She says you're lucky, but you know that.
She asks you if you lost consciousness—you tell her "no."
She leaves to consult with a neurologist.
You wait.

The maintenance worker comes back to empty the trash.
He says hello again.
He smiles at you.
He offers to turn out the light as he leaves.
You thank him, tell him the light is fine as it is.
You smile at him.
You wait.

The doctor returns.
She says you don't need a head CT.
She says she'd like to keep you under observation for a few hours.
You tell her you want to go home.
She says you can do so if you can walk,
if you can keep fluids down without vomiting.
As she leaves she says she'll send the nurse back in.
You wait.

The nurse returns,
gives you some pills for your headache,
some water to swallow them down.
She asks if you're ready to take a walk.
You tell her yes, ask her if you can walk in the direction of a bathroom.
You need to pee.
She laughs, walks you to the bathroom,
points out the call button on the wall in case you need help.
You don't need help.
When you open the door again, she's gone.
You walk back to your room, surprised you remember where it is.
The hospital corridors are confusing.
You wait.

A different nurse comes.
She says your nurse is on break.
She looks at your chart.
She asks if you've been to CT yet.
You tell her the doctor said it wasn't necessary.
You tell her the doctor said you could go home.
She leaves to check with the doctor.
You wait.

The new nurse comes back.
She reads you a lot of instructions.
She hands you the instructions.
She tells you that you can get dressed and go.

5. Grace

You get dressed.
You call a friend to pick you up.
You walk out of your room,
ask the nurse at the desk if there's anything you need to sign,
anything you need to do before you go.
She says "no."
You ask her how to get out.
She points you towards the lobby.
No one questions you as you leave.

You walk out of the hospital.
It's only four hours since the accident.
It's a beautiful afternoon—
brilliantly sunny, breezy,
green and blue and gold.
As you wait for your friend,
you feel an overwhelming sense of grace.

Mining the Ore

Women are walking
hip to hip,
their bellies emptied of children,
their hands slapping their flat thighs
rhythmically.

And look—
there is your mother.
Her wounded eyes no longer hold your perfect image.
If you open her veins
gold will flow, singing.

And look—
there is your sister.
Her small feet no longer hush
for the perfect sound of your first steps.
If you open her veins,
gold will flow out, singing.

And look—
here am I, a woman
like your mother, like your sister.
My shattered hands no longer wait
for the rain of your perfect tears.
If you open my veins
gold will flow like honey, singing.

We are walking hardfoot together.
Our hands slap our flat thighs
rhythmically.
We are chanting the names you never gave us,
our bellies still loose,
slack as a cat,
but emptied now of you.

Vera Nazarov

Balancing Act

> *Since morning*
> *she has fallen fathoms—*
> *dropped like a plummet*
> *through net after net*
> *of care...*
> —Ril Lovell, *Mad Girl*

Rope dancer—
every step a gamble between
slip and surefoot,
balance and disaster.

She's been up there, it seems,
forever—
rosin long worn off her aching soles.
Her toes cramp;
the flat muscles of her calves,
the long muscles of her thighs,
stiffen—brittle as old wood.

She can no longer feel it—
the true north of perpendicular—
down the center of her spine.
She starts to sway,
uncertain of upright.
In a few brief hours,
perhaps days,
maybe a week,
she may be dead.

Oh hold her close,
this child, this woman,
this heartflung creature,
this baby girl.
She dances perilously close
to the end of all things,
to the edge of the world

.

Tethys

The Visit

Mary, my mother, sits on the edge of her bed,
stares at the ceiling,
rattles off a phrase or two of Russian,
rocks back and forth rubbing her hands over her knees,
clockwise, then counterclockwise.
Her eyes wander the room, come to rest on me—a recognition.
I see her thought in her eyes—proud, possessive:
"This is mine. I made this!"
She says to a passing nurse *"Eta moia dochka."*
Met with a blank look, she repeats in English
"This is my daughter."

Distracted again by the ceiling,
she turns her gaze upward once more, listening.
Then the body calls, and she ponderously rises,
lumbers over to the potty chair,
hikes up her garish purple dress and sits,
thighs pancaking across the seat,
pale and flabby as over-risen bread dough.
She concentrates, strains,
attention turned inward,
and is rewarded by a "plop, plop."
She flashes me a look, a smile—triumphant achievement.
As she wipes, she relates to me this morning's conversation with my father
(dead these twenty-five years of a brain tumor),
and tells how the Virgin Mary,
as a special favor to her,
moved the Cathedral of the Annunciation from Moscow
to Burlingame.

Mary, my mother, blessed with daily miracles,
dwells in the odor of sanctity in this urine-reeking rest home.
As she happily prattles on
I reflect on the chaos of my childhood—
then I didn't know this word: *schizophrenia.*
Now each visit is a lesson in forgiveness
and I am a conscientious student.

I rise to go.
I tell my mother goodbye.
I say I'll come again soon.
I kiss her slack cheek.
In her mind I'm gone already.
She smiles timorously at this stranger,
then her eyes are drawn heavenward again.
As I leave, she's conversing with angels.

Feathers

> *Hope is the thing with feathers*
> *That perches in the soul...*
>   —Emily Dickinson, *Hope*

My grandfather slept behind curtains.
This is what my mother always told me.
As a child, I imagined a lush four-poster bed
draped and canopied in rich velvets and brocades
in the room I wasn't allowed to enter—
the room in which my grandparents slept.
I later learned she meant
he was old-fashioned in his thinking.

We lived in a small room behind the kitchen
at the back of my grandparents' flat
in the avenues of San Francisco—
Richmond District, with its Russian delis and bakeries
and Easter midnight mass at
Holy Virgin Cathedral.

The living room where my grandmother
watched *One Life To Live, Search For Tomorrow, Guiding Light*,
struggling to understand through her thick Russian,
languished in shadow:
heavy drapes at the windows
protected the heavy dark furniture from sunlight,
sad-eyed icons lingered high in the corners,
unframed pictures covered every inch of wall—
pictures by my grandfather's son,
my uncle, the artist:
charcoal sketches of long-dead faces,
muted watercolors of rainy city streets,
faded memories of distant places.

I was all about magenta and aquamarine and spring-green
from my bright orange 64 Crayolas box.
We drew pictures together, my mother and I:
fantasy landscapes of hills like green breasts,
a golden quarter sun with rays like spokes
peeping in from the corner,
and at the topmost edge of the paper,
a line of improbably blue sky.

Vera Nazarov

Mother's love of color did not end with my crayons.
Shopping with her was a downtown adventure into
bright geometrics and brilliant paisleys,
hippie florals like blobs in a lava lamp—
dresses too hideous to contemplate
from the vantage of the enlightened twenty-first century.
To my unjaded eyes they were beautiful.

Grandfather did not approve.
"These are colors for young girls,"
he told my mother.
"Widows and women with children
dress modestly, wear dark colors.
You are acting ridiculous,
setting a bad example for your daughter,
bringing shame on the family.
Stop dressing like a whore!"
Mother didn't listen, didn't care.
Every shopping trip ended in shouting and tears,
bitter recriminations, unforgivable words.

Her final-straw dress was a cute little just-above-the-knee number
(she had the legs for it, in her pearly three-inch pumps):
bright spring-green linen, cap-sleeved,
jaunty little collar with its
tie-shaped dangle of fabric,
wedge-shaped edge capped in brass.
After the inevitable round of shouting,
grandfather ripped the dress from mother's hands,
flung it in her face.
The tie's metal edge opened a crimson line on her forehead;
spots on the dress spread red against green—
poppies blooming in a summer field.
Grandfather took mother to the hospital in a taxi,
yellow cab shining like the spoke-rayed sun,
to have her head stitched.
Soon after, we moved out.

Single-motherhood and depression
will eventually wear down
even the most persistent dreamers.
Mother, still a young woman
in her shapely mid-thirties,
with her technicolor America-dreams,
became drab and shabby
despite her clothes—
thin and worn and tired,
her red-lipsticked mouth crumpling like wet silk
into my grandmother's
enduring anxious frown.

Older now than she was then,
I choose to remember her glad laughter,
bursting on the air like tickle-me bubbles.
I still dream in the colors she gave me,
magenta, aquamarine, spring-green
running behind my eyes like melted crayons.
I still believe in her
improbably blue skies.

Selfish Child

A memory...
The end of a rainy schoolday,
first grade, Star of the Sea Elementary,
water droplets making snail-trails down tightly shut
impossibly tall windows,
steamy with the wool-uniform damp of
thirty squirming little bodies.
Sister leading us in song—
not "Hail Holy Queen" but unaccountably, "Swanee River."
I sang "Way down the 'Ponaswanee' River, far, far away..."
Then coats and galoshes and my mother at the door:
foldout plastic rain kerchief tied under her chin,
covering her sparse gray hair, pink dandruff-flaking scalp,
wet cloth coat, snot green with big ugly khaki buttons,
thick support hose,
sensible brown shoes down at heel—
beautiful in the end-of-the-day eyes
of a tired first-grader.

It never occurred to me to wonder
what my mother did all day while I was at school.
She didn't work,
wasn't much of a cook or housekeeper,
not a reader either, and we had no television,
no radio even.
I imagine her going home to our
silent apartment,
making a cup of tea,
sitting quietly then, like a discarded doll
until it was time to collect me.

I would ask her if I could...
Was the silence restful without my brash, noisy,
self-important six-year-old presence?
What did she think about?
What did she remember?
My father, dead when I was three of a brain tumor?
The war that scattered shattered families?
Born in 1929, she would have been a child of twelve
during Operation Barbarossa,
the Axis invasion of the Soviet Union.

Mariya,
youngest child,
only girl,
called by everyone Marusa,
smiles out of sepia family photographs
in her too-short skirt—
photographs in which no one else smiles.
But the photographs have faded,
the edges nibbled away by mice,
images eaten by damp and time.

Memories waver like watery reflections
disturbed by a thrown stone.
I return to my mother, alone in our empty apartment
and I realize that I'm still that selfish child,
unable to imagine my mother without me.

Wearing My Mother's Face

Her perpetually worried frown,
anxious eyebrows,
mouth tight, firmly set against
another of life's little surprises,
did not prepare me for that look—blank,
too shocked for shock:
my mother's face when she emerged from the bathroom...

We were going to a dinner party
(strangers, acquaintances, distant friends)
I would be the only child present—
my precious, precocious, six-year-old self,
pressed and primped to make her proud.
She prepared me first:
sky blue dress, clouds of white lace,
new (clean) white tights,
black unscuffed patent leather shoes...
hair freshly out of the horrible,
hard-as-rocks-to-sleep-on,
pink plastic curlers,
combed until I could scream (and did)
just so.

Directed then to sit quietly, read a book,
until she was ready—
bored, tired, cranky,
mad,
I got her razor from the dresser,
shaved off my eyebrows.

Nothing to be done, we had to go.
The invitation had been accepted.
No punishment,
no amount of shaking, tears or recriminations
would grow back my eyebrows within that final hour,
could turn me into a good child, a better daughter.
Still, there was that mad flutter of momentary hope:
"this isn't real!"

All My Oceans

It's that look that haunts me—
that first second of stunned disbelief,
as if freezing like a deer in headlights
could turn back the clock, make it not true,
make it all right—
that look, and the fact that I inspired it,
that I was glad.
Now I surprise that same look sometimes,
in the morning, in the mirror.
In a karmic joke, I wear my mother's face.
If I shaved them off again, I wonder,
incurred my own share of that shame,
would that settle the debt?

Things Fall Apart

> *Things fall apart, the center cannot hold...*
> —William Butler Yeats, *The Second Coming*

My mother at sixty was all woman:
broad hips, thick thighs,
breasts still round (softness subtly running to slack).
You could imagine she made love,
woke in the night sometimes with trembling limbs,
a slow curl of heat in her belly.
Now she looks like a boy:
stick-skinny, neck to ankles;
her voice, once warm and throaty, rises reedy and thin.
She doesn't look anymore at the hills she once strode
with our dogs (Ebony, Arrow, Lady and Belle)
in their wild elliptical orbits around her.
She was the center around which we all fell,
shrinking so slowly and quietly we never noticed
the encroaching dark, her fading warmth.
She's been sifted by time and tide to the finest particles;
worn down from use like a fine knife honed keen
until all that remains is edge.

She is a fire sinking slowly to embers
and I wonder how her final going out will affect us all.
Will we drift apart, no longer held in our proper paths,
weaving and crashing into each other?
Will we continue in our blind orbits
not realizing our focus is gone?
Will we fall into her absence and disappear?
Hard to say, but we hold this one thing in common:
none of us can move to the center
and hold the rest together.
We're too noisy, too fragile, too self-centered.
All afraid to burn—unwilling to give
light and warmth impartially.

Still, I wish she could go out like she lived,
in one giant rending supernova,
one final burst of heartlight burning us all new,
sending us off in directions not of our choosing.

A Gift of the Heart

> And I have something to expiate:
> A pettiness.
> —D.H. Lawrence, *Snake*

November.
We were in Woolworth's, my mother and I
in the back of the store
amid needles and notions,
the pet department chattering and burbling
two aisles to the left.

In among the cushions and the curtains
a sleekly oiled and barbered man
was promoting gimcrack jewelry at a rickety table
draped in threadbare blue beneath the display boxes.
He made a grand show of seating mother on a
folding metal chair
before rattling into his sales patter.
I stood behind her, beguiled by the ripple of words,
breathless before the bangles and baubles.

She bought a necklace—
a rather pretty gold-washed affair
with a flower made of stones which were not diamonds.
It cost something-ninety-nine.
The salesman informed her that
for the investment of one further penny
(bringing the total to something-even)
she could also have their promotional jewelry item,
a gold-washed serpentine chain with
tiny golden teardrops at its ends
and a zipper pull (also gold-washed)
that slid up and down the chain,
making it adjustable, like a bolo tie.

My teenage heart went out to that necklace—
it was cute, it was unusual, it was shiny.
I asked on the way home if I could have it.
Mother said no,
that she was giving it to my sister for Christmas.

Later that day I told my sister
not what her Christmas gift would be,
but knowing how price-conscious she was,
how much it cost,
determined that if I couldn't have the necklace,
she wouldn't enjoy it.
On Christmas day, I watched as she unwrapped her gift.
Her protestations of thanks rang with great sincerity;
only I could hear the sneer.
She never wore the necklace.

All these years
I thought we were so different,
my mother, my sister and I.
But even though we did it each in our own way,
we had all begrudged a gift of the heart.

Anchor

Somewhere I've never been,
somewhere I've seen only in dreams,
on the edge of sleeping and waking,
you wait to take my small
starfish hand
in your hard grainy hand
and teach me again
how to crimp a line,
how to wrap it twice around and through the notch,
how to set the bait and cast the hook
far and deep.

Your eyes crinkle against the sun
as we watch the silver sinker spiral down.
The tiles are slippery under my sneakers—
slick with blood,
pink and black with fish guts
that get caught in the filters,
but you,
you could never fall,
could never fall away.

This is the way I want to remember you:
tall, golden,
your dark head haloed with light
as I look up and up,
forever up to the sun
which never forgets.

My Father's Kitchen

transmission fluid stored in an old syrup bottle
a drawer full of vegetable seeds escaped from their packets
a loaf of bread and some bananas in the dishwasher
tools
odd bits of machinery
bibs and bobs of electrical wiring
cords from long-burnt-out electric fry pans
five bottles of liquid smoke for making beef jerky
    "because it was on sale"
a hoof pick one of us kids left outside
a snaffle bit from a worn-out bridle
packets of shoelaces
tins of shoe polish
a pair of legless eyeglasses
sheetrock nails
finishing nails
bolts
washers
duct tape
fresh and spicy summertime salsa
all our Thanksgiving and Christmas dinners
and way down in the icy dark bottom of January
a simmering pot of homemade chicken soup

Several Attempts at a Funerary Poem

People say all the wrong things at funerals...
"He was a great husband and father," and all that crap.
No one ever says "My dad could spit like a sniper."
or "He wasn't prejudiced—he hated everybody."
No one ever says the really true things.

*

The hands that knew how to shape a piece of wood,
how to take apart and reassemble anything mechanical,
how to handle tiny blind kittens
are folded and still.
These hands that never in life lay folded and still like that,
these hands want something to do.
Give them a hammer
and they'd look more comfortable.

And that gentle, peaceful smile—
he never in his life smiled like that!
His was the evil puckish grin,
gleeful in its malevolence,
laughing at the world's foolishness.

*

We still feel his presence,
like the ghost pain of an amputated limb.
He has left a hole in our lives
that the days wash over
but never quite fill.

Day by day the echo of his voice in the walls grows fainter.
A day may finally come
when I can walk through the house
and simply admire the fine grain in the wood
without necessarily remembering working side by side with him,
laying down the squares...
the afternoon sunlight swarming with dust motes
and the smell of his sweat,
musky and huge,
seeping into my skin.

The blood heat of his living presence in the house cools,
becomes background static,
primal white noise.

*

I am writing this same poem over and over.
Eventually, I will get it right.

I will never get it right.

Father

> ...your anvil
> of anger
> my dread
> of your danger—
> spilled cauldron of anguish...
>   —Ryl Lovell, *The Sword*

> Daddy, daddy, you bastard, I'm through.
>   —Sylvia Plath, *Daddy*

It won't do anymore, you know,
packing you away with the flotsam and jetsam
fragments of a fractured childhood.
The frail bulkheads,
delicate rigging—
ship of my soul, my self—
splintered and wrecked on your rocky obdurance
where I only saw, only sought,
safe harbor.

This the one half of life with you:
Lustful eye that followed,
watched, waited until I was alone,
fearful, wary.
The too intimate, too personal caress...
the over-prolonged kiss...
the crude jokes,
sly insinuations,
never enough to cry foul, to point blame—
all innocent,
and I the confused,
the misunderstanding,
the lying child.

This the other half:
Towering rages,
glacial silences,
the thousand small hurts,
calculated to sting and sting and sting—
your army of wasps—
each one crafted to pierce sensitive skin,
burrow deep into unprotected flesh,
hooked and barbed so that
pulling them out would be more painful
than their first strike.

And yet still, rare moments of kindness,
of humor, of camaraderie;
moments of a love so wished for that
when you died, I truly grieved…
cruelest joke of all.

Rusalka

A Little Heart to Heart

> *He that made this knows all the cost,*
> *For he gave all his heart and lost.*
> —William Butler Yeats, *Never Give All The Heart*

So here we are again,
just you and me again, my old heart.
Pull up a chair, order a beer…
you don't have to tell me, I know:
shot down again,
handed the mitten,
returned like an unwanted gift.
I tried to tell you before…
only the pretty girls,
the mean cruel ones,
ever win at this game,
but you don't listen—
foolish optimist;
you insist on keeping that damned
thing with feathers alive and singing.
Given a choice, I'd drown it.

Janis Ian tried to tell us
At Seventeen…
here we are now,
decades later,
considerably older but no wiser,
still waiting to be asked to dance,
still aching to spend all our tenderness on
some poor jerk who will never deserve it.

It's okay, go ahead and cry.
Get it out of your system before the next
unfeeling asshole
walks in through that door.

Persephone and Hades

You accepted the pomegranate he offered, Persephone,
coyly glancing beneath lowered lashes.
As you grasped the shattered half-globe—
light-scattering ruby-glamoured geode—
your fingers delicately brushed against his wrist.
The six seeds you swallowed stained your pale lips crimson.

You let him unbind your hair then, Persephone,
and his hand trembled as he stroked its rich gold.
You mesmerized him with your midsummer eyes—
his eyes, shadow-deep, dark with troubled secrets,
followed you as you stepped softly through his rooms,
as you turned again into his embrace,
the deep copper of your summer skin,
the rise and fall of your breast with each breath,
warm against his marble pallor.

You knew what you wanted, and you took it—
give to him now what you promised.

A New Hester Prynne

She pauses in the dim light of the fireplace,
draws the newly folded laundry to her face,
presses her cheek to a pill-knotted sweater.
In the other room, the child is sleeping,
quick breath loud in the pounding silence.

She turns to the window, considers her reflection,
eyes dark as the shadows behind her,
dark as the woods behind the glass,
dark as this darkest night of the year.

Her lover praised her eyes first,
then stripped her to her soul,
cataloging every curve, every hollow,
in a never-ending cycle of praise.
His urgent murmurs rose like incense on the air
as he worshiped esculent flesh,
filled her with prayers and psalms
and the shudder of his ecstasy.

All facades were shattered that night.

Tears slip down her cheek as she considers the darkest sleep
for her and her lovely mistake.

Vera Nazarov

Innocent Love Is Easy Love

We were two, innocent as children,
purely loving, freely trusting,
and we were one—heart, mind, soul.
Innocent love is easy love.

Love flew without a net then,
rare air its element,
until it fell,
a missed handclasp and it
plummeted
to earth.

I ran to save it,
knelt to gather it up, hold it close,
but even as I strove to hold, to mend,
the pieces shattered in my hands,
cruel shards, friable as glass,
tearing my flesh,
making me bleed.

Two could have saved it—
two pairs of hands, working together—
but you turned your back, walked away,
left this precious, this innocent thing
lying broken in my
torn and bleeding hands.

I cried out to you in a voice of anguish.
You never looked back,
your silence, your indifference,
an arrow to my heart.

Love after pain, after grief,
comes harder, stumbles,
chafes in rough clothes,
learns trust again slowly, in lessons of fire,
of blood,
overcomes pain, but never forgets,
understands love is pain...
love breeds pain.

I am still there, in that place,
still kneeling,
still holding this shattered, this beautiful thing
in my hands
as it slowly fades, collapses, dies,
crumbles away into shimmering dust
mixed with my blood and my tears.

I will mold it into a new shape,
never as beautiful as in its innocence,
but a strong shape, a vessel
to pass through fire and become
more than its elements—
a chalice into which I will pour
my heart's blood, my silver tears,
the shining essence of my self,
the vibrant flame of my life.

I will offer it—a libation
to the one who comes in thirst,
to the one who comes in need,
to the one who comes seeking,
to the one who sees me.

Ghosts

Millions of tears cried, yet
I've still to reach
the bottom of that ocean.

How can a piece of meat,
elegant pump of muscle and blood,
feel like it's being torn to pieces
simply because you've turned away?
I trusted you to know that
I love you without fear,
without mercy,
with all my sins,
all my mistakes.
Now I am homeless,
a bag lady,
pushing my cart of
shattered promises,
empty words,
abandoned dreams.

There's a hole in my heart
where the tears run in.
There's a space between my arms
shaped just like you and
my arms are lonely,
longing to hold you
The weight of this longing
presses down on my chest and
I can't catch
my breath
for wanting you.

Throw my heart to the dogs.
Let the crows take my eyes.
I will lose myself in the space between
white emptiness and
black abyss—
deepest darkness of my secret sins,
ugliness that no one can love,
loneliness crying—a stray cat at the door.

Blackest midnight was radiant with your light.
White noon is shadow dark without you:
a pool of clinging, sucking blackness where
the child in me drowns and dies,
leaving behind another ghost of me...
the ghost I thought you loved.

Falling

A falling stone,
a falling shower,
the falling call of a wren
are hardly recompense for the falling shower of leaves
chestnut and golden against this drab ground,
this bowl of dreary cloud.

I lean my forehead against the window,
cold this November day.
The only green thing in sight,
a straggling orange tree,
bravely clinging to its leaves
against the chill wind,
the heavy sky.

I remember the sound of the door,
the heavy click of the latch
loud in the falling stillness,
the silence that came flooding in
to fill the space you left behind.

You were the rolling stone,
the one falling stone
that begins the avalanche,
and rolls out unscathed at its end.
When we met, I began falling.
I am falling still now you've gone.

Boundaries

> *though i have closed myself as fingers,*
> *you open always petal by petal myself as Spring opens*
> *(touching skilfully,mysteriously)her first rose*
> —e.e. cummings, *somewhere i have never traveled,gladly beyond*

The map of yourself that you share with the world
is a palimpsest, obscured with cautionary phrases:
> *terra incognita,*
> *terra periculosa,*
> *hic sunt dracones...*

borders of uncharted territory teeming with warnings:
> *be mindful of the boundaries,*
> *do not stray off the edges.*

But the one who loves you
is no respecter of such barriers.
She will fly past the public *"you"*
seeking that which is real, that which is hidden:
your soft, vulnerable underbelly,
the tender heart you conceal so desperately,
all your broken and bleeding places—
touching so softly, mending so quietly,
you may not even notice at first
the initial sighing breath of warm air,
infinitesimal pink blush of sunrise,
gradual opening of a carpet of wildflowers,
delicate green of returning spring,
in the long winter,
dark, frozen wasteland,
Ultima Thule of your heart.

Vera Nazarov

Mask

> *We wear the mask that grins and lies,*
> *It hides our cheeks and shades our eyes, —*
> *This debt we pay to human guile;*
> *With torn and bleeding hearts we smile...*
> —Paul Laurence Dunbar, *We Wear The Mask*

This mask I wear...
I began building it the first time my heart broke.
Portions of it are coldly beautiful, but mostly it's a
grotesque, composed of eccentric angles,
planes that follow bizarre contours,
made to disguise an all-too-human thinness of skin,
shield the vulnerability of a human heart that feels
too much, too deeply.

My mask has been carefully crafted of
words that wound,
cruel barbs of old heartache,
every dark and terrifying thing that ever
crawled from my midnight soul.
I built it deliberately, artfully,
strengthened it with ancient resentments,
torn and bleeding edges of shattered dreams,
the banshee shriek of a drowning solitude.
But the stronger it grew, the more it turned inward,
its intricate defenses spearing skin flayed raw,
inflicting an agony greater than the sum of its parts.

I've worn this mask so long now it's bone-fused,
spikes and spalls penetrating
fragile ear and cheek and collar bones.
Heavy and cumbersome,
it drags down my head,
shutters my eyes...
Removing it is so excruciating,
I don't even try anymore.

It has extruded its own scaffolding—
struts and spars of rusty rebar, the color of dried blood—
buttressing itself against back and chest and shoulders.
One jagged spur, crimson-black,
grows in an arc towards my heart;
one day it will slowly, inexorably, impale that delicate organ,
delve its way through warm living flesh,
render that precise animate metronome
cold and still and soundless.
On that day the mask will prevail—
tightly clasped around my skull,
solidly fused across my eyes, my mouth,
it will leave me blind and silent as old stone.

You could see the *me* behind my mask,
with a single touch, make it vanish.
If you wanted to, you could see me.

Closed Circuit

Love set me going in the beginning,
and in my baby steps I walked the path
that spiraled out from childhood.
Every circuit brought new vistas,
fresh fields,
friends and lovers.
Some walked with me for a while,
some left too soon;
each altered my trajectory,
sent me into unknown territory.

A few placed stones in my path...
planted thornbushes.
I cleared the path each time,
moved the stones aside,
dug out the thorns.
My hands grew rough and scarred,
but I spiraled out yet again,
always seeking the new path...
the fresh adventure.

There came a time though when
turning back into an old path,
closing the circuit,
seemed easier.
The stones grew too big,
the thorns too dense for my strength alone.
Bowed down, I could no longer see that
help was a handclasp away...
I only had to reach out.

Now I circle the same path again and again,
avoiding the obstacles.
The path is worn, smooth and dusty,
soft and comforting to my feet;
I know every inch of it intimately,
like a lover's body,
but with every circuit it grows darker
as its walls rise up on either side.
First ankle high, then knee, hip, chest, shoulder...
I've worn it so deep now, I no longer see beyond it.
Its earth is filled with the fossilized remains of
ancient heartaches.
It lies open before me; I have the
illusion of freedom—
I tell myself I'm going somewhere.
The deception comforts me,
but the walls rise higher and higher,
gradually close in around me.
A little light leaks in from above, but
I don't look up anymore.

Sometimes, more and more rarely,
a voice tickles my ear,
a hand reaches down into my trench,
offering help to climb out.
I keep my head down,
plod doggedly on…
I no longer trust such illusions.
My path grows darker.
The light is a lie.

Vera Nazarov

Incarnate

> *I like this strangely you know,*
> *this quiet dark-eyed ship I will sneak on*
> *quietly as a dewdrop & then away*
> *I'll be where the real **there** is, but*
> *women, sometimes I think they're*
> *not profound enough to die.*
> —Alice Notley, *September's Book*

There will come a day,
not overly strange,
and not undyingly bright,
when I will up anchor
and lift sail into the gathering dark
at the horizon,
letting the low light fall as it will
behind me.

I shall run before the wind,
run to the wind's twelve quarters,
with the long light
and the sun, low and golden,
falling westward.

I shall be golden as the sun
when I return out of the long dark
and you shall greet me as stranger,
shall not remember me
except faintly, as the sound of distant bells
or the brief animal glow of eyes
on a country road at dusk.

But your heart will know me then
as I am now, and be mystified.
I shall be a poem you almost wrote,
music half-remembered,
beautiful with the wind
and lost as Persephone
in the paths of the unmourned dead.

The Brutal Gentleness of Regret

You will hear thunder and remember me,
And think: she wanted storms.
   —Anna Akhmatova, *You Will Hear Thunder*

There is nothing I can't hide
Save for the memory.
   —Gordon Peterson, *Save For the Memory*

When the rains resume, as you understand they must,
after the last golden days have melted away,
when naked trees rub together chapped hands, crackling fingers
over the final fading glimmer of Indian summer,
you will sit on your porch in the deepening twilight,
and remember how autumn inspired her smile.

In the black pre-dawn of winter,
when you awaken to brittle silence, icy hardwood,
bone-deep chill of short gray days,
you will pull on warm hand-knit socks
and recall her surprising denial of sunrise.

Spring's fragile green,
bitter fragrance of new life,
will reverberate like subtle thunder,
entangling, ensnaring your desire;
trees in bud, blossoming flowers,
will flicker, flamelike, on the edges of your vision,
taking the shape of wounds on the world,
and you will rise up in the despairing dark of midnight,
randomly thinking: pink…she liked pink.

In the midsummer dusk, as furnace heat mellows,
unyielding edges of day soften and fade,
the scent of parched meadow grasses will envelop your senses,
a woman's gentle laugh will ripple forth like cool water
through the open windows of a neighboring house,
linger on still, breathless air…
Then the soft murmur of another voice,
her voice: low and warm, caressing,
the line of her throat,
cascading curl of her hair —
sunlit, tousled, windblown,
as she tossed her head back in delighted laughter —
will torment your memory.

Moonbeams will spill softly
through serene leaves, peaceful trees.
There will be a golden glow of lamplight,
white curtains fluttering on a fan's manmade breeze,
rich perfume of coffee, oven-warm pie…
The silken air of evening will caress your skin,
its touch as soft and fragrant as her hands.
You will turn back, slowly retrace your steps,
return to all your ghosts,
the echoing shadows of your empty room,
alone.

Index of Titles

5 May 2010, 69
Ambulance, 71
Anchor, 91
Babies, 34
Balancing Act, 76
Ballet Russe, 66
Barren, 29
Beauty, 11
Becoming the Sun, 43
Borders, 36
Boundaries, 107
Brutal Gentleness of Regret, The, 113
Castles in Spain, 32
Cat's Snooze as an event in spacetime, The, 53
Cernunnos, 26
Chameleon, 5
Clocks, 67
Closed Circuit, 110
Collision, 69
Delta, 62
Dreaming of Red, 8
Echoes, 6
Equinox, 47
ER, 72
Eucalyptus, 61
Falling, 106
Father, 95
Feathers, 81
Feet, 42
Fisherman's Wife Writes to Her Friend, The, 38
Fishing, 31
Four Seasons Kanji, 49
Fruta Prohibida, 21
Ghosts, 104
Gift of the Heart, A, 89

Grace, 74
Grapes, 33
Gravity, 10
Hair, 35
Heat, 7
Here, Now, 17
Horse Daydreaming in a Sunny Field, 48
How Love Comes, 9
ICU, 40
Incarnate, 112
Innocent Love is Easy Love, 102
Juice, 22
Kiss, 19
Learning a Foreign Language, 37
Little Heart to Heart, A, 99
Mask, 108
Migraine, 52
Mining the Ore, 75
My Father's Kitchen, 92
New Hester Prynne, A, 101
Old Bones, 41
On the Shoulder, 70
On Your Shore, 3
Persephone and Hades, 100
Places Seldom Kissed: A Litany, 24
Quilters, The, 60
Rain, 50
Rain, 54
Riding the Horse, 65
Saturday Morning in the Group Home, 64
Selfish Child, 84
Several Attempts at a Funerary Poem, 93
Stained, 15

Stone in a Temple Wall, 56
Submission, 20
Tangerines, 51
Things Fall Apart, 88
Things You Miss: A Litany, 23

Today My Name Is… , 59
Visit, The, 79
Wearing My Mother's Face, 86
Zen Garden, 55

Index of First Lines

A falling stone, 106
A memory…, 84
A million individual, 50
Beneath the moon, beneath the trees, 8
"Chameleon," he said, 5
Fingertips, 24
For you alone…, 20
He stands too still for me to perceive, 26
Her perpetually worried frown, 86
How the tongue struggles at first, 37
Hunched over in the dusty California sunlight, 33
I came from a mountain quarry, 55
I know that I am not beautiful, 11
I never wanted one, 34
I was becoming used to this serene emptiness—, 29
I'm a fragment of river, 48
I've never been to Spain, 32
ice-cold from the fridge, 51
Infinite blue dome;, 9
It is here that I wait for you always, 17
It is sometimes a barrier, 35
"It needs a gardener,", I thought, 54
It won't do anymore, you know, 95
It's like waking up, 31
Kiss…kiss me…, 19
Love set me going in the beginning, 110

Mary, my mother, sits on the edge of her bed, 79
Millions of tear cried, yet, 104
Morning cracks, 52
My grandfather slept behind curtains, 81
My mother at sixty was all woman, 88
Nibbler of minutes, 53
November, 89
Now it is time for bluebells to sleep, 47
Old bones, you have danced, 41
People cross borders, 36
People say all the wrong things at funerals…, 93
Purpling like a bruise, the sky sleeps, 67
Rope dancer—, 76
Round sound of plum:, 21
She pauses in the dim light of the fireplace, 101
So here we are again, 99
Somewhere I've never been, 91
Summer hills—, 7
Sunlight dripped slowly, thick honey, 22
Suppose your body was an ocean:, 3
The bottoms of your feet are soft and blind, 42
The fourteen-year-old boy who raped a six-year-old girl, 64
Ragged thunderheads, 65
The lion that lives in your garden, 43

The map of yourself that you
     share with the world,
     107
The nurse at the admit desk
     asks for your medical
     record number three
     times, 72
The officer comes back, 70
The paramedics walk you to the
     ambulance, 71
The scented morning teases you
     awake:, 10
The sharp gasp she makes at
     your first thrust, 23
The way my sister lolled at
     poolside:, 62
There is room tonight, 61
There will come a day, 112
This mask I wear…, 108
To be stained, 15
Today my name is Heart's
     Thunder, 59

transmission fluid stored in an
     old syrup bottle, 92
Try to move me one inch I do
     not choose to move, 66
Voices beamed into space, 6
We move like needles, 60
We were two, innocent as
     children, 102
When the rains resume, as you
     understand they must,
     113
wildflowers, grass, trees—, 49
Women are walking, 75
You accepted the pomegranate
     he offered, Persephone,
     100
You asked in your last letter, 38
You can see it's inevitable, 69
You get dressed, 74
Your body no longer belongs to
     you:, 40